THANK YOU FOR YOUR CONTIN

Published By My Littl' Workshop

To purchase additional
copies of this book, go to:
www.MyLittlWorkshop.com

MY NOTEBOOK

NAME:

CONTACT:

YEAR:

GIFT FROM:

EMERGENCY:

OTHER INFO:

I AFFIRM THAT:

I am a boss and I'm okay with myself.

I am a winner and I'm okay with myself.

I am a genius and I'm okay with myself.

Today is the day of my amazing manifestation.

Everyday I make miracles, and I'm okay with myself.

Miracles follow miracles in my world.

I am forever grateful, thank you Most High!

- Rev. Dr. Marie Brevil

SistaTokblog

What's up for

TODAY?

PUT YOUR BOSS PICT HERE.

SOMETIMES, YOU HAVE TO SEE YOURSELF AS YOU WISH TO BE.

What's up for
TODAY?

What's up for

TODAY?

What's up for TODAY?

What's up for TODAY?

What's up for
TODAY?

What's up for TODAY?

What's up for

TODAY?

What's up for TODAY?

What's up for TODAY?

What's up for TODAY?

What's up for

TODAY?

PUT YOUR BOSS PICT HERE.

SOMETIMES, YOU
HAVE TO SEE
YOURSELF AS
YOU WISH TO BE.

What's up for TODAY?

What's up for TODAY?

What's up for TODAY?

What's up for TODAY?

What's up for TODAY?

What's up for

TODAY?

What's up for

TODAY?

What's up for
TODAY?

What's up for TODAY?

What's up for TODAY?

What's up for

TODAY?

PUT YOUR BOSS PICT HERE.

SOMETIMES, YOU HAVE TO SEE YOURSELF AS YOU WISH TO BE.

What's up for TODAY?

What's up for TODAY?

What's up for TODAY?

What's up for TODAY?

What's up for TODAY?

What's up for

TODAY?

What's up for TODAY?

What's up for TODAY?

What's up for TODAY?

What's up for TODAY?

What's up for

TODAY?

PUT YOUR BOSS PICT HERE.

SOMETIMES, YOU
HAVE TO SEE
YOURSELF AS
YOU WISH TO BE.

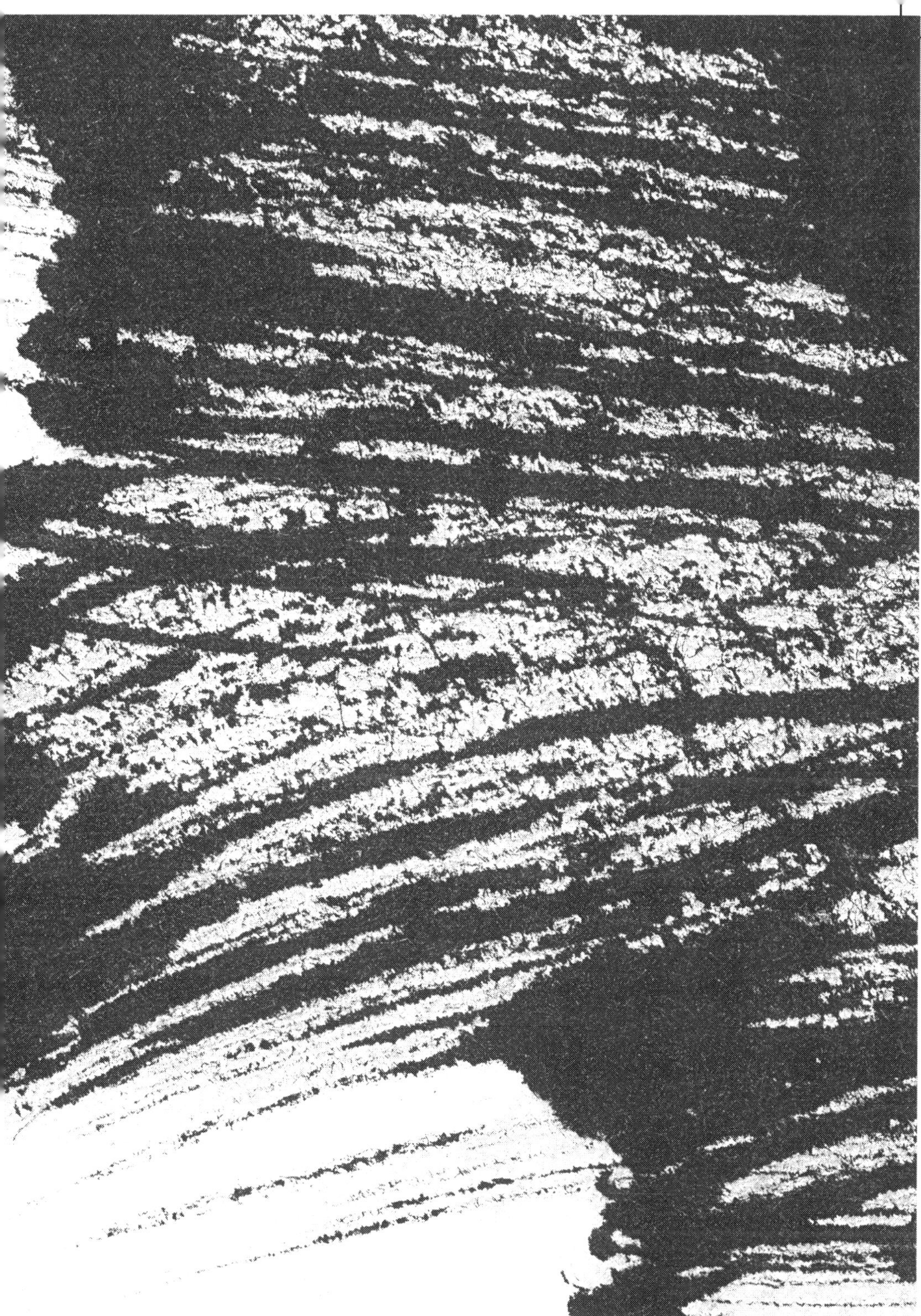

What's up for

TODAY?

Boss Mov

What's up for

TODAY?

Boss Move

What's up for
TODAY?

Boss Mov

What's up for

TODAY?

Boss Move

What's up for

TODAY?

Boss Mov

What's up for

TODAY?

Boss Move

What's up for

TODAY?

Boss Mov

What's up for
TODAY?

Boss Move

What's up for

TODAY?

Boss Mov

What's up for

TODAY?

Boss Move

What's up for

TODAY?

PUT YOUR BOSS PICT HERE.

SOMETIMES, YOU HAVE TO SEE YOURSELF AS YOU WISH TO BE.

What's up for TODAY?

What's up for TODAY?

What's up for TODAY?

What's up for TODAY?

What's up for TODAY?

What's up for

TODAY?

What's up for

TODAY?

What's up for TODAY?

What's up for TODAY?

What's up for
TODAY?

Money moves

What's up for

TODAY?

PUT YOUR BOSS PICT HERE.

SOMETIMES, YOU
HAVE TO SEE
YOURSELF AS
YOU WISH TO BE.

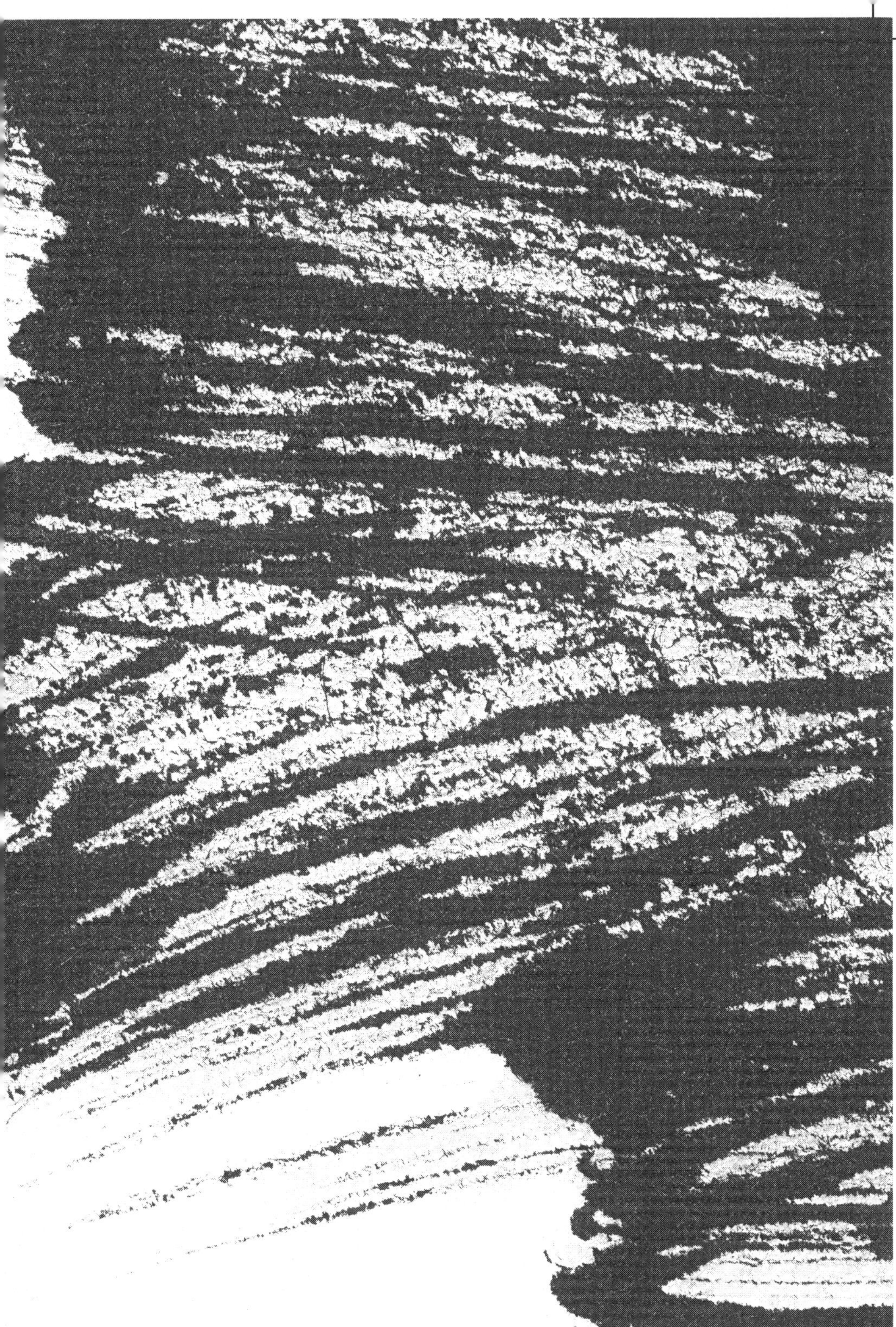

What's up for TODAY?

Winning Mindset Always!

What's up for TODAY?

Winning Mindset Always!

What's up for TODAY?

Winning Mindset Always!

What's up for TODAY?

Winning Mindset Always!

What's up for TODAY?

Winning Mindset Always!

What's up for TODAY?

Winning Mindset Always!

What's up for TODAY?

Winning Mindset Always!

What's up for TODAY?

Winning Mindset Always!

What's up for TODAY?

Winning Mindset Always!

What's up for TODAY?

Winning Mindset Always!

What's up for

TODAY?

PUT YOUR BOSS PICT HERE.

SOMETIMES, YOU
HAVE TO SEE
YOURSELF AS
YOU WISH TO BE.

What's up for
TODAY?

What's up for TODAY?

What's up for

TODAY?

What's up for
TODAY?

What's up for TODAY?

What's up for TODAY?

What's up for
TODAY?

What's up for

TODAY?

What's up for TODAY?

What's up for

TODAY?

AFFIRMATION FOR A BOSS LIKE ME.

I am a boss and I'm okay with myself.

I am a winner and I'm okay with myself.

I am a genius and I'm okay with myself.

Today is the day of my amazing manifestation.

Everyday I make miracles, and I'm okay with myself.

Miracles follow miracles in my world.

I am forever grateful, thank you Most High!

- Rev. Dr. Marie Brevil
SistaTokblog

What's up from

NOW ON BOSS?

Stay boss

NOW TO FOREVER!

AFFIRMATION FOR A BOSS LIKE ME.

by Mari[illegible]evil

What's up from

NOW ON BOSS?

Stay boss

NOW TO FOREVER!

AFFIRMATION FOR A BOSS LIKE ME.

by Mari[illegible] evil

What's up from

NOW ON BOSS?

Stay boss

NOW TO FOREVER!

AFFIRMATION FOR A BOSS LIKE ME.

by Mari[illegible]evil

I PROMISE MYSELF THAT:

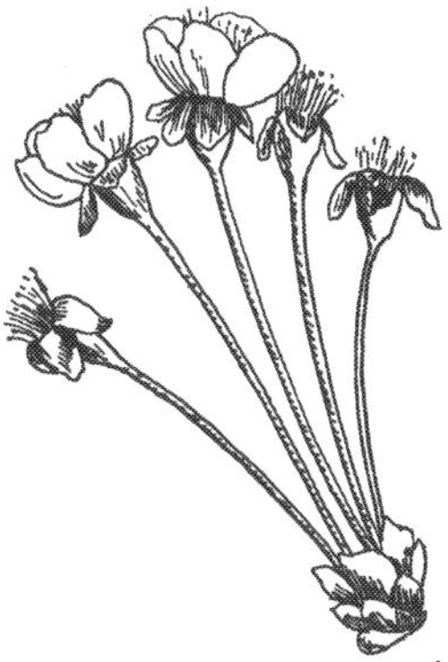

I PROMISE MYSELF THAT:

I PROMISE MYSELF THAT:

Made in United States
Orlando, FL
04 November 2026

90218655R00055